The ABCs of Being Greek

An A-Z Journey Through Greek Culture From Athens to Zorba

Helen Christina Kyrillidis

REF NUMBER: 25724281125S046

Copyright © 2025
DOLLARS AND SENSE PUBLISHING, LLC
The ABCs of Being Greek:
An A-Z Journey Through Greek Culture
From Athens To Zorba
All rights reserved.

No portion of this book may be reproduced, distributed, or transmitted in any form or by any means without written permission from the publisher or author, except in the case of brief quotations embodied in critical reviews and certain other non-commercial uses as permitted by U.S. copyright law.

DOLLARS AND SENSE PUBLISHING, LLC
New York, NY

Printed Worldwide
First Printing 2025
First Edition 2025

DISCLAIMER:

Some elements of Greek culture have been simplified to help young readers. All Greek words are spelled using standard modern Greek conventions. The content of this book has been derived from various sources. Illustrations were created with a combination of hand-guided design, digital art tools, and AI-assisted artwork. Please note the information contained within this document is for educational and entertainment purposes only. All effort had been executed to present accurate and complete information.

"You Know the Greeks Invented That…Right?"

So much of today's world can be traced back to Ancient Greece.

In fact, even the word "**alphabet**" comes from the first two letters of the Greek alphabet, **Alpha** (Α, α) and **Beta** (Β, β).

Many words come from Greek roots. For example, let's take the word "**astronaut.**" It combines **"astron" (ἄστρον)**, meaning "star" and **"nautes" (ναύτης)** meaning "sailor." So, an astronaut is a "star sailor" - someone who sails through space, just like sailors travel the seas.

Another example is the word "**geography**." It comes from the Greek words **"geo" (γῆ)** meaning "earth" and **"graphein" (γράφειν)** meaning "to write or describe." So, geography means "writing about the earth!"

If you take a closer look at many words and break them up, you'll find that over 50% of the English language comes from the Greek language! Many words we use every day, like telephone (tele = "far" and phone = "voice"), democracy (demos = "people" and kratos = "power"), and microscope (micro = "small" and scopein = "view"), have Greek origins. So…Surprise! You already speak some Greek!

In addition to language, the Greeks made huge contributions to science, math, philosophy, art, architecture and so much more. Greek ideals and words have traveled through history and are still a big part of the world today!

But this book isn't just about words. It's here to introduce you to the amazing world of Greek culture! From delicious foods and lively dances to ancient myths and beautiful islands, Greece is full of history, traditions, and fun. So, get ready to explore **"The ABCs of Being Greek"** and discover what makes Greece so special!

A

Athens (Αθήνα) is the capital of Greece and one of the oldest cities in the world. It is full of history, culture, and amazing food. High above the city stands the **Acropolis (Ακρόπολη)**, which served as the religious heart of Ancient Athens. Even though it was built thousands of years ago, many of the buildings still stand today and people come from all around the world to visit it daily.

The Acropolis includes the famous Parthenon which was built to honor the goddess **Athena (Αθηνά)**. In fact, the city of Athens was named after her. She is usually depicted in statues wearing a helmet and holding a spear as she was the goddess of war and strategy.

The sparkling **Aegean Sea (Αιγαίο Πέλαγος)** is the bright blue water that surrounds Greece and is home to many of its beautiful islands.

Throughout the world, everyone knows the Greek soup called **avgolemono (αυγολέμονο)**. It's very name gives up the two main ingredients eggs (αυγό) and lemon (λεμόνι). Add in chicken and orzo (or rice or a very thin noodle called fide), and you get avgolemono! The eggs and lemon are mixed together to make the soup creamy. It's enjoyed on cold days or when someone isn't feeling well. Warm, comforting and full of delicious lemon flavor, it's a classic taste of Greece!

B

Baklava (μπακλαβάς) is probably the most well known Greek dessert. It's made with layers of crispy phyllo dough, nuts, and a sweet honey syrup. It's a delicious treat that you'll find at almost every Greek celebration!

One of the most beautiful sounds is the sound of the **bouzouki (μπουζούκι)**, a traditional Greek musical instrument that fills the air with lively melodies. It can make people feel many different emotions. The notes from a bouzouki can sound happy, excited and even sad.

And of course, no talk about Greece is complete without mentioning the colors of **blue and white (γαλανόλευκο).** You can see them on the Greek flag and on the bright white buildings with blue roofs, windows and doors on the islands. When these buildings are set against the deep blue sea and sky, they create a picture-perfect scene that shows the true beauty of Greece.

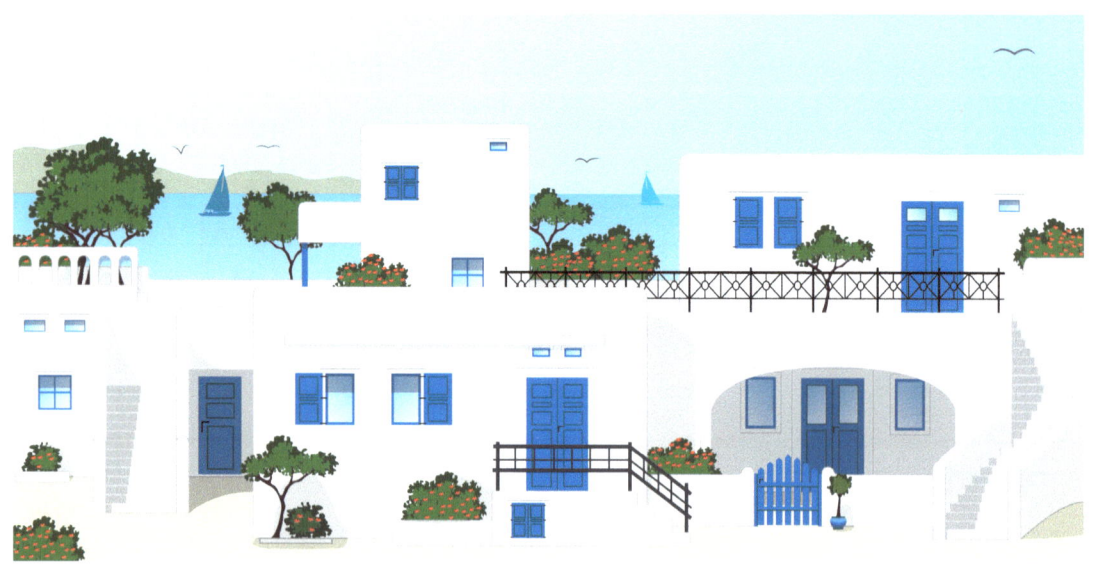

C

Ancient Greece is famous for its grand **columns (στήλες)**, which held up their buildings and temples. Some of them, like the ones on the Parthenon, still stand even today throughout Greece despite being built over 2500 years ago.

Greece is home to many beautiful islands, each with its own charm:

Corfu or Kerkyra (Κέρκυρα), covered in lush green hills and buildings, is known for its history and breathtaking beaches.

Crete (Κρήτη), the largest Greek island, was home to the ancient Minoans and the famous palace of Knossos, where the legend of the Minotaur was born.

Then there are the **Cyclades (Κυκλάδες)**, a group of islands famous for their white houses, blue-domed churches, and like all of the Greek islands, crystal-clear waters. The beautiful islands of Mykonos and Santorini are part of this island chain.

D

The ancient Greeks gave the world **democracy (δημοκρατία)**, a system of government where people have power, they vote and make decisions about how to run their country. Most countries use this system still today. In a democracy, everyone's vote counts and people are free to share their ideas.

Dolmades (ντολμάδες) are a popular Greek dish. They are grape leaves stuffed with rice and herbs. And for something sweet, there's **diples (δίπλες)**, a crispy, golden fried pastry drizzled with honey and topped with walnuts and cinnamon.

The **drachma (δραχμή)** was the country's currency for over 2,500 years before Greece switched to the Euro in 2002.

Greece is also home to many beautiful island groups, like the twelve known as the **Dodecanese (Δωδεκάνησα)**, which includes islands such as Rhodes and Kos, filled with historic sites, like medieval castles, and of course, crystal-clear waters and breathtaking beaches and coves.

E

Greece itself is called **Ellada (Ελλάδα)** in Greek.

In Greek culture, many people believe in the **Evil Eye (Μάτι)**, a superstition that says too much envy or admiration can bring bad luck. To protect themselves, Greeks wear blue glass charms shaped like an eye or hang them in their homes.

One of the most famous Greek treasures are the **Elgin Marbles** or the **Parthenon Marbles (Γλυπτά του Παρθενώνα)** a collection of ancient sculptures that were once part of the Parthenon in Athens but are now displayed in the British Museum in London, England.

Many Greeks hope that one day these beautiful pieces of Greek history will return to their home in **Ellada**!

F

Greece is famous for **feta (φέτα) cheese**, a delicious, crumbly white cheese made from sheep's milk or a combination of sheep and goat milk. Often seen in blocks or in cubes, it's used in Greek salads, pies, and many traditional dishes. In the summertime, it is also enjoyed with watermelon!

Greeks also love to celebrate, and throughout the year, there are many **festivals (πανηγύρι)** filled with music, dancing, vendors, and amazing food. These festivals sometimes celebrate a religious holiday, a local saint, or an important cultural event in a village. Many churches around the world celebrate their Greek heritage by hosting festivals once a year and people of all backgrounds are welcome to enjoy the delicious Greek food, learn the dances, and experience Greek culture!

At many of these festivals, and at cafes and beaches throughout Greece, one can enjoy a **frappe (φραπέ)** - a popular iced coffee made with instant coffee, water, sugar and milk, shaken or blended until frothy. It doesn't matter what season it is, this refreshing beverage is popular all year long!

Faki (φακή) and **fasolada (φασολάδα)** are two cozy Greek soups that families have enjoyed for many, many years. Faki is a warm lentil soup, and fasolada is a tasty white bean soup. Both are healthy, simple meals that give you lots of energy.

In the Greek Orthodox Church, many families **fast (νηστεία)** during certain times of the year. Fasting means choosing simpler meals without meat or dairy. Faki and fasolada are often eaten during fasting days because they are filling and do not include any ingredients that would break the fasting traditions.

Fasting is most often done in preparation to receive Holy Communion. The Eucharist, another word for Holy Communion, is a very special moment in the Greek Orthodox Church. During the Divine Liturgy, the bread and wine are blessed and become the Body and Blood of Jesus. The people receiving communion walk slowly to the priest with their hands at their sides, open their mouths carefully, and treat this moment with respect because it is holy.

An important value in Greece is **filoxenia (φιλοξενία).** It comes from the Greek words "filos" (φίλος) meaning "friend" and "xenia" (ξενία) meaning "stranger" so it literally means "friend to strangers." It is the Greek tradition of warm hospitality, welcoming guests with open arms and treating them like family.

But the most important Greek value is one of **filotimo (φιλότιμο)**. While this translates to "friend (or love) of honor," it is a word that cannot be easily explained or defined. It means so many things like honor, integrity, compassion, humility and encompasses having a love for life, doing the right thing and helping someone in need without expecting anything in return. The best way to explain it is simply this: it is a way of life for Greeks all around the world.

G

Galaktoboureko (γαλακτομπούρεκο) is a popular dessert, made with creamy custard tucked between layers of flaky phyllo dough, then baked and soaked in a sugary syrup. It's sweet and soft with just the right amount of crunch and usually served warm. Greek families love serving it during holidays or after a big Sunday meal.

A **gyro (γύρος)** is one of the most popular street foods in Greece. It is made up of thin slices of seasoned meat, usually pork, chicken, lamb, or beef, stacked on a large, vertical spit. The spit slowly turns on a rotisserie, cooking the outer layer evenly. As the meat turns, the outside becomes crispy. Once the outer layer is cooked, it's sliced off with a sharp knife in thin, tender strips. And then the process begins all over again with the next layer as the gyro keeps turning. And even though it's spelled with a "g," it's pronounced as "yee-ros"

While the ancient Greeks worshipped Greek gods, today most Greeks follow the **Greek Orthodox Church (Ελληνορθόδοξη Εκκλησία)**, which plays a big role in their traditions, celebrations, and daily life. The leader of the Greek Orthodox Church worldwide is the Patriarch. Each area has a Bishop and larger areas have an Archbishop.

H

Greece is also known as **Hellas (Ελλάς)**, the name Greeks use for their own country.

Of course, Greece has islands and big cities, but it also has many small villages, called a **horio (χωριό)**, where life is full of tradition and community. In a horio, you don't just know your next door neighbors, you know everyone who lives there. It's the kind of place where doors are always open and everyone waves when they drive or walk by.

Greek mythology tells the stories of gods and heroes. One such hero is **Herakles (Ἡρακλῆς),** who was known for his bravery. He's most famous for his incredible strength and for completing twelve impossible tasks, called the Labors of Herakles, like fighting a lion and capturing a boar. His stories are about courage, strength, and never giving up.

The island of **Hydra (Ὕδρα)** is a special place in Greece. It is a completely car and motorcycle free island (except for emergency services) where the mode of transportation is either walking the cobblestone streets with your own two feet or hitching a ride via donkey or mule.

I

Another group of islands are ones in the **Ionian Sea (Ιόνιο Πέλαγος)**. The Ionian islands, like Corfu, Kefalonia and Zakynthos, are on the west coast of Greece known for their lush greenery and of course, once again, like so many of the Greek islands, crystal-clear waters and picturesque scenery.

Greece is also home to incredible stories, like those found in **The Iliad (Ἰλιάς)**, an epic poem by Homer that tells many stories like the tale of the Trojan War and the adventures of the mighty Greek warrior heroes, Achilles, Agamemnon and Odysseus.

In Greek Orthodox churches and homes, people display **icons (εικόνες)** which are beautiful religious paintings that are an important part of the Greek Orthodox faith. The **iconostási (εικονοστάσι)** is a special place in a home where these religious icons are displayed. There is a deep connection between everyday life and the Orthodox faith in Greek culture.

And every year on **Independence Day (25η Μαρτίου)**, March 25th, Greeks around the world, celebrate their freedom with parades, by wearing traditional costumes and waving flags, remembering the start of the Greek War of Independence in 1821. That was when the Greek people stood up to the Ottoman Empire and began fighting for their freedom after centuries of rule.

J

In ancient Greece, athletes competed in the **javelin throw (ακοντισμός)**, a sport in the Olympic Games where they hurled a long spear as far as possible. The **javelin (ακόντιο)** was not only used in sports but also in battle. Greek warriors carried these spears as weapons.

In Greek Orthodox churches, you may see the **Jerusalem Cross (Σταυρός της Ιερουσαλήμ)**, a large cross with four smaller Greek styled crosses, representing Christianity spreading to the four corners of the world.

K

In Greece, people start their day with a warm **"Kalimera" (Καλημέρα)**, which means "Good morning!" And it's traditional to wish others a **"Kalo Mina" (Καλό μήνα)** or "Good Month" on the first of every month.

Καλημέρα

Two of the most loved and traditional cookies in any Greek home are the **Koulourakia (κουλουράκια) and Kourabiedes (κουραμπιέδες).** They are usually baked before Christmas, Easter, or big family gatherings, filling the house with a warm, sweet smell.

Koulourakia are light, buttery cookies often shaped into braids, spirals or little S-shapes. Families love making them together, rolling the dough and shaping each cookie by hand. They are usually brushed with egg to give them a golden shine and sometimes topped with sesame seeds.

They're gently sweet, a little crunchy, and perfect for dipping into coffee, milk or hot chocolate.

Kourabiedes are melt-in-your-mouth cookies covered in a snowy blanket of powdered sugar. They're made with a lot of butter and often have roasted almonds inside, giving them a rich flavor and a little crunch.

When you take a bite, the powdered sugar can puff everywhere and make a big mess, but that's part of the fun of eating kourabiedes!

A **komboloi (κομπολόι)**, is a string of worry beads that helps people pass the time and relax. Many elders can be found at the local **kafenio (καφενείο)** or café twirling around a komboloi.

Greeks are also known for their **kefi (κέφι)**, a special word that means joy, excitement, and a love for life especially when dancing, singing, and celebrating with family and friends.

And, there's **Karagiozis (Καραγκιόζης)**, the funny and mischievous character from a traditional Greek shadow puppet theater show who entertained generations upon generations of Greek children.

L

If you ever visit Athens, be sure to climb up **Lycabettus Hill (Λυκαβηττός)**, the highest point in the city, where you can see breathtaking views of the Acropolis, all of Athens and the sea beyond.

A favorite Greek treat for people of all ages, young and old, are **loukoumades (λουκουμάδες)**, small, golden honey puffs that are crispy on the outside and soft on the inside.

A **lambada (λαμπάδα)** is a large decorated candle, traditionally used during Easter. On Holy Saturday night, people attend church, and at midnight, they light their lambada from the Holy Light, symbolizing the resurrection of Christ. These candles are often beautifully decorated, especially for children, with ribbons, small toys, or religious symbols.

M

Greece is famous for its incredible **mythology (μυθολογία)**, filled with stories of powerful gods, brave heroes, and magical creatures. These myths tell the tales of powerful Greek gods who all lived on **Mount Olympus (Όλυμπος)**, the tallest mountain in Greece, where Zeus, the King of the gods ruled.

The word **marathon** **(μαραθώνας)** comes from an ancient Greek story about a soldier, Pheidippides, who ran all the way from the town of Marathon to Athens to announce a battle victory. Upon reaching the city, he exclaimed "We have won!" and then collapsed from exhaustion. This inspired the modern marathon that we see in the Olympics today.

Marathons are also run in cities all over the world, including the Boston Marathon, the New York City Marathon and the Athens Authentic Marathon which is held in Greece every year. The Athens Authentic Marathon covers the same route that Pheidippides took over 2500 years ago, starting in Marathon and ending in Athen's Panathenaic Stadium, where the first modern Olympics were held in 1896 and which is built entirely out of white marble.

After all that running, you would definitely be hungry, and in Greece, a delicious meal like **moussaka (μουσακάς)**, is the perfect comfort food. It is a layered dish of eggplant, potato, and meat, topped with a layer of béchamel, a creamy white sauce that is soft and fluffy.

And for a comfort dessert, nothing beats **melomakarona (μελομακάρονα)**, soft, sweet cookies that are soaked in a warm honey syrup and topped with chopped nuts. Their spicy aroma makes them especially popular during Christmas.

Molon Labe (Μολών Λαβέ) means "Come and take them!" and was said by the Spartan King, Leonidas. A long time ago, a powerful king named Xerxes told the Spartans to give up their weapons. But Leonidas, said "Molon Labe!" meaning, "If you want them, come and take them yourself!" Even though his army of 300 was small, Leonidas and his brave soldiers fought to their death to protect their land. It's a reminder of the Spartan spirit, sacrifice, and bravery.

N

In modern Greece, one of the most stunning places to visit is **Navagio Beach (Ναυάγιο)**, also known as "Shipwreck Beach," in Zakynthos with its pristine waters and a famous shipwreck resting on the white sand.

Name days (Ονομαστική εορτή) are very special in Greek culture and are celebrated just like birthdays, sometimes even more so than birthdays! Many Greek names come from saints, and each saint has a special day on the church calendar. When that day arrives, people celebrate everyone who shares that name. On a name day, family and friends call, visit, or send good wishes, and the person being celebrated may offer treats or open their home to guests. Some families even have a small gathering or meal together.

On someone's name day, people usually say **Xronia Polla (Χρόνια Πολλά)** which translates to "Many Years," but what it really means is "May you live a long, healthy life and celebrate many happy years to come! "

Here are some popular Greek name days and the names that are celebrated on those dates.

Date	Names Celebrated
January 1	Vasilis, Vasiliki, Basil
January 6	Fotis, Fotini
January 7	Ioannis, Ioanna
January 17	Antonios, Antonia
January 18	Athanasios, Athanasia
January 25	Gregorios
February 10	Charalambos
March 25	Evangelos, Evangelia
April 23	Giorgos, Georgia
May 5	Eirini
May 21	Konstantinos, Konstantina, Eleni
June 29	Petros, Pavlos
July 17	Marina
July 20	Elias
July 26	Paraskevi
August 6	Sotirios, Sotiria
August 15	Maria, Panayiotis, Panayiota
August 30	Alexandros, Alexander
September 14	Stavros, Stavroula
September 17	Sophia, Elpida, Agapi, Pisti
October 18	Loukas
October 26	Dimitrios, Dimitra
November 8	Michael, Gabriel
November 25	Katerina, Catherine
December 4	Barbara
December 6	Nikolaos, Nikos, Niki
December 7	Anna
December 12	Spyridon
December 15	Eleftherios, Eleftheria
December 25	Christos, Christina

In Greek mythology, **Nike (Νίκη)** was the powerful goddess of victory, symbolizing success in both war and competition. Her name even inspired the famous sports brand!

The Greek gods were said to drink **nektar (νέκταρ)**, a magical drink that gave them immortality and endless energy.

O

The **Olympics (Ολυμπιακοί Αγώνες)** began in ancient Greece over 2,000 years ago, where athletes from different city-states competed in sports like running, wrestling, and javelin throwing. Today, the modern Olympic Games continue to bring people together, but now from all over the world. Athletes compete for gold, silver and bronze medals. And because Greece is where the Olympics first began, at every Opening Ceremony, the Greek team is always the first to enter the stadium, the Greek flag is raised and the Greek national anthem is played. It's a moment of great pride for all Greeks.

Greece is also famous for its delicious **olives (ελιές)**, which have been grown for thousands of years and are used to make rich, golden olive oil.

After a meal, some adults enjoy a glass of **ouzo (ούζο)**, a traditional Greek drink with the strong taste of anise, often sipped slowly while chatting with friends.

No Greek celebration is complete without a loud **"Opa!" (Ώπα!)** - a joyful shout often heard during dancing, music, and fun moments.

Ohi Day (Επέτειος του Όχι) is celebrated every year on October 28th to remember a brave moment in Greek history. On this day in 1940, during World War II, Italy, led by a man named Mussolini, told Greece to let Italian soldiers come in and take over. The Greek Prime Minister at the time, Ioannis Metaxas, gave a strong answer: "Ohi!" (Όχι), which means "No!" in Greek. This strong "No" showed the world that the Greek people would stand up and fight for their freedom and independence.

P

In the heart of Athens, on the Acropolis, stands the **Parthenon (Παρθενώνας)**, an ancient temple dedicated to the Greek goddess, Athena, the city's namesake and protector.

Just below it lies **Plaka (Πλάκα)**, a charming Athens neighborhood with narrow streets, colorful houses, and small shops where you can find traditional Greek souvenirs.

The sea god **Poseidon (Ποσειδώνας)** was one of the most powerful Greek gods, ruling over the oceans with his mighty trident. Many of the Greek myths tell stories of his adventures and battles.

When it comes to food, Greeks love to eat **pita (πίτα)**, a soft, round bread used for wrapping sandwiches like gyros or dipping into tzatziki.

Pastitsio (παστίτσιο), is a baked pasta dish with layers of ground meat, creamy béchamel sauce, and delicious spices. It is often called the "Greek Lasagna." Many people consider it their favorite Greek dish.

Pappou (Παππούς) is the Greek word for grandfather. He's always telling stories from long ago, teaches us traditions, and always greats us with a big smile and hug.

Many Greek families used to live in a beautiful place by the Black Sea called **Pontus (Πόντος)**. These **Pontian Greeks (Πόντιοι Έλληνες)** had their own Greek dialect, lively music, quick dances, and treasured places like the Panagia Soumela Monastery, a breathtaking church built in 386 AD high on a cliff and in a mountain. Their special traditions are still celebrated today, keeping the spirit of Pontus and Pontic Hellenism alive with a Panagia Soumela in Vermio Greece and one in New Jersey in the United States.

Q

Greek mythology is full of dramatic stories, including the famous **quarrels of the gods (Διαμάχη των Θεών)**, where the powerful gods fought and argued over land, power, and honor. One great quarrel was between Zeus and Prometheus, when Prometheus defied Zeus by giving fire to humans, leading to a harsh punishment.

In ancient Greece, chariot races were an exciting sport, where skilled riders controlled a four horse chariot, a **quadriga (τέθριππον)**, or tethrippon, speeding through grand competitions.

Many ancient Greek stories tell of heroes who went on daring **quests (αποστολές)**, including Odysseus, whose long journey home after the Trojan War was filled with challenges, from facing the Cyclops to escaping the wrath of Poseidon.

The Greeks also valued **questioning (αμφισβήτηση)**, which started with great philosophers like Socrates always asking "Why?" to better understand life. Some famous Socrates' quotes include "I cannot teach anybody anything. I can only make them think." and "Wonder is the beginning of wisdom." When we are curious and ask questions, we can learn new things and become smarter every day.

R

During Greek Orthodox Easter, families celebrate with a special tradition - **red eggs (κόκκινα αυγά)**! The eggs are dyed deep red to symbolize new life and the resurrection, and people play a fun game called tsougrisma, where they tap their eggs against each other to see whose will stay uncracked the longest.

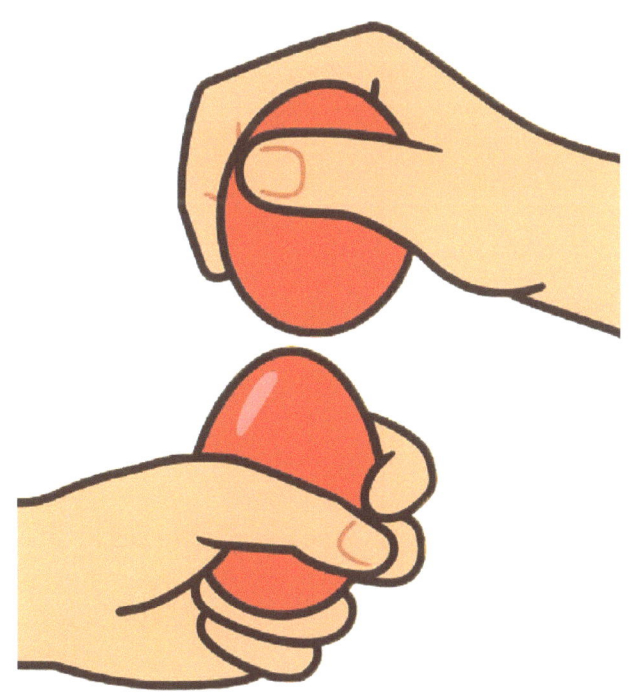

In Greek music, a **rebetis (ρεμπέτης)** is a musician who plays rebetika, a soulful style of folk music often called the "Greek blues," filled with songs about life, love, and hardship.

And no Greek feast is complete without a glass of **retsina (ρετσίνα)**, a traditional Greek white wine with a unique resin flavor that has been enjoyed for thousands of years.

S

Music and dancing are a big part of every celebration, such as weddings, christenings, birthdays, and namedays. One of the most famous dances is the **Sirtaki (Συρτάκι)**. In this dance, people stand in a line and gently place their hands on each other's shoulders. They begin with slow steps, but then the music gets faster and faster, and everyone's feet try to keep up!

After all that dancing, it's time to eat delicious Greek food! One of the most popular treats is **souvlaki (σουβλάκι)**, which is tender pieces of grilled meat on a wooden skewer. You can eat it right off the

stick, or tuck it into warm pita bread with tomatoes, onions, and creamy tzatziki sauce. The smell of souvlaki cooking on street corners is so good that it's almost impossible to walk by without buying one!

Another tasty Greek favorite is **spanakopita (σπανακόπιτα)**, also called spinach pie, a golden, crispy pastry filled with spinach, herbs, and feta cheese. Each layer of phyllo dough is thinner than a sheet of paper, but when it bakes, it becomes light and crispy. Spanakopita can be baked in big pans which is then cut into pieces or folded into little triangles as an individual treat.

And then there's **saganaki (σαγανάκι)**, a thick slice of kaseri or kefalotyri cheese that is covered in flour and then fried until it turns bubbly and golden. Sometimes, especially in restaurants, the cheese is set on fire right before serving! Then lemon is squeezed on it to put the fire out and you're left with warm, melty cheese in a crispy outer shell.

When it comes to history, no Greek city was as tough and brave as **Sparta (Σπάρτη)**. Spartan boys were taught to be strong, disciplined, and courageous. Their tough training began as early as age 7! They learned to run fast, work as a team, and never give up. That is why Spartan warriors were known throughout the ancient world for their power and skill.

T

Thessaloniki (Θεσσαλονίκη) is Greece's vibrant second-largest city, and it is known for its rich history, lively culture, and iconic seaside promenade. One of its most recognizable landmarks is the White Tower (Λευκός Πύργος), which once served as part of the city's defense walls. Today, it stands proudly on the waterfront as a symbol of the city and houses a museum dedicated to Thessaloniki's history. The White Tower is a beloved photo backdrop and a place to soak in panoramic views of the Thermaic Gulf. Surrounded by cafés, street musicians, and sunset strolls, it represents the spirit of Thessaloniki: a blend of the old and new, and always full of life.

Throughout towns and cities like Thessaloniki, you'll find many **tavernas (ταβέρνες)**. A taverna is a great place to enjoy traditional food, mostly appetizers, like grilled octopus and fried calamari, grilled meats and seafood, with friends and family. It's more than a restaurant. People gather there to eat, drink, laugh, and perhaps even listen to some live music.

Of course, no Greek meal is complete without **tzatziki (τζατζίκι)**, a creamy yogurt dip with cucumber and garlic, perfect for dipping grilled meats like souvlaki and gyro and for spreading on warm pita bread.

Another tasty food is **tyropita (τυρόπιτα)**, or cheese pie, made with flaky phyllo dough and a creamy cheese filling. Most Greek families pass down this recipe from generation to generation.

Tsoureki (τσουρέκι) is a sweet, braided Greek bread that's soft and chewy. It can be eaten all year long but is mostly popular at Easter, either as a loaf or a ring shape. It is sometimes baked with a bright red egg in the middle.

A **tsolias (τσολιάς)**, is a Greek soldier wearing a white kilt-like garment known as a foustanella, red shoes with pom-poms, and a beautifully embroidered vest. This was the traditional uniform of the Greek fighters during the War of Independence. In today's Greece, they are members of the Presidential Guard and are also known as Evzones. As members of this group, they guard the Tomb of the Unknown Soldier and every hour, perform a solemn Changing of the Guard ceremony. On occasion, they also travel and visit Greeks that live outside of Greece, to participate in various ceremonial duties and parades and to promote the Greek culture.

U

In ancient Greece, people used large jars called **urns (αγγείο)** to store valuable things like olive oil, wine, water, and honey. Sometimes they were used during special ceremonies. These urns were often beautifully decorated with symbols, scenes from daily life or stories about the gods. Many of these ancient urns have been discovered by archaeologists and are now displayed in museums around the world for everyone to admire.

The **Upper Town (Άνω Πόλη)** of Thessaloniki is like a city above the city. It's the oldest and highest part of Thessaloniki, filled with narrow cobblestone streets, colorful houses, and old stone walls from the Byzantine era. Upper Town feels like stepping back in time, surrounded by history on every corner.

Greece is home to many mysterious **underground caves (Υπόγειες Σπηλιές)**, like the famous Melissinos Cave in Kefalonia. Visitors go there and wait on long lines to take a boat ride through the cave and enjoy the crystal-clear and calm waters up close.

In Greek culture, **unity (ενότητα)** has always been important, from the ancient city-states coming together to fight common enemies to extended families coming together for holidays and celebrations today. Greeks are known worldwide for having strong family bonds. The Greek diaspora, Greek people who live outside of Greece, even join organizations based on the village, island, or region their family comes from, to stay connected to their roots no matter where they live.

V

In northern Greece, the city of **Vergina (Βεργίνα)** is where archaeologists discovered the grand tomb of Philip II, the father of Alexander the Great, revealing treasures from Greece's glorious past. The Vergina Sun, which was Alexander the Great's symbol, has 16 rays said to represent the 4 elements (earth, fire, air and wind) and the 12 Greek gods of Mount Olympus. It was designated as an official national symbol by the Greek Parliament in 1993.

In modern history, **Eleftherios Venizelos (Ελευθέριος Βενιζέλος)** was one of Greece's most important leaders, helping to shape the country into what it is today. He served as Prime Minister seven times and is said to be the "Maker of Modern Greece." Even though he died in exile in Paris, his body is laid to rest on a hilltop in his hometown of Chania, Crete. There are many statues of him throughout Greece and even one in Washington D.C., outside the Greek embassy.

Every New Year's Day, Greeks celebrate with **vasilopita (βασιλόπιτα)**, a special cake with a hidden coin inside. Whoever gets the piece of cake with the coin in it is said to have good luck for the year ahead!

According to tradition, during the 4th century in the city of Caesarea in Cappadocia, the local governor demanded that the people who lived in the city give him their gold and valuables. St. Basil the Great, who was the Bishop of Caesarea, urged the governor to repent. The governor changed his mind and gave all of the treasures he had collected to St. Basil to give back to the people.

But St. Basil had no way of knowing which item belonged to whom, so he had the treasures baked into one big loaf of bread. He blessed the bread and as he cut and distributed pieces to the people, each person miraculously received their own valuables back.

W

In ancient Greece, a **wreath (στεφάνι)** made of olive or leaves was placed on the heads of Olympic champions, symbolizing victory and honor.

The Ancient Greeks loved **wine (κρασί)**, which was an important part all of their feasts and of their religious ceremonies. They even had a god of wine, Dionysus!

Another great value in Greek culture is **wisdom (σοφία)**. The goddess Athena, in addition to being the goddess of war and strategy, was also the goddess of wisdom. In some illustrations, she is seen with an owl by her side, because an owl is a symbol of wisdom.

She guided heroes and philosophers, like Socrates, Plato and Aristotle, in their search for knowledge. Wisdom means using your heart and your brain to make good choices. It helps people solve problems, share with others, and learn from mistakes.

In Greek families, grandparents and older people are often listened to because they've learned a lot over the years. Their advice is seen as being very special because they are full of wisdom.

X

In Greece, the name **Xristos (Χρήστος)** is very common, but it can also mean "Christ" when the emphasis is on the last syllable (**Χριστός**)

On December 25th, Greeks celebrate **Xristougenna (Χριστούγεννα)**, the Greek word for Christmas! When we break down the word, it comes from the Greek words "Xristos" (Χριστός) meaning "Christ" and "genna" (γέννα) meaning "birth." So, Xristougenna means "the birth of Christ." During this time, families gather to enjoy traditional foods and sing carols (called kalanda), to celebrate the holiday season.

On Easter Sunday, and for 40 days afterward, Greeks around the world greet one another with **"Xristos Anesti" (Χριστός Ανέστη)**, meaning "Christ is Risen." The traditional response is "Alithos Anesti" (Αληθώς Ανέστη), which means "Truly, He is Risen."

There is also a special hymn sung in church at a midnight liturgy on Easter Sunday and said as a prayer for those 40 days:

"Xristos Anesti ek nekron,
thanato thanaton patisas,
kai tis en tis mnimasi,
zoeen harisamenos."

which translates to:

"Christ is risen from the dead,
trampling down death by death,
and to those in the tombs
bestowing life."

After the midnight service, Greek families gather at their homes to celebrate with a joyful feast. The table is filled with magiritsa (a traditional Easter soup), sweet tsoureki, and of course, bright red eggs.

The next day, on Easter Sunday, Greek families gather outside to cook lamb slowly on a spit over an open fire. The lamb turns and roasts for hours, filling the air with delicious smells while family and friends laugh, dance, and wait together. Sometimes they even pick at the meat as it turns as a taste test of the meal to come! When it's finally ready, it's time to sit down and eat all together.

Y

Greece has a rich history of heroes and one of them was **Demetrios Ypsilanti (Υψηλάντης)**, a leader in the Greek War of Independence who fought bravely for freedom. The city of Ypsilanti, Michigan, US, founded in 1823, during the Greek struggle for independence, is named after him! And a bust of him stands between a Greek and a US flag at the base of the landmark Ypsilanti Water Tower.

But Greek culture isn't just about warriors, it's also about family and traditions. Every Greek family has a beloved **yiayia (γιαγιά)**, or grandmother, who fills the house with warmth, wisdom, and delicious home-cooked meals and desserts.

Another popular food Greece is famous for is **yogurt (γιαούρτι).** Thick and creamy, it is often served with honey and nuts as a healthy and tasty treat or dessert.

Yiasou (Γεια σου) is a Greek saying that translates to wishing someone good health but is also used to say hello, goodbye, or cheers. You'll hear it when people wave hello, say goodbye, or clink their glasses together. Greeks say **Yiasou** to friends and family or the plural form of the word, **Yiasas (Γεια σας),** to elders or groups. They even use it to say "Bless you" when someone sneezes.

Z

In Greek mythology, **Zeus (Ζευς)** was the most powerful of all the gods, ruling from Mount Olympus with his mighty thunderbolt. He was the king of the gods and the god of the sky, storms, and lightning. Many myths tell how he protected people, kept order among the gods, and made sure the world stayed balanced. But don't get him angry, because then he would throw thunderbolts, shake the sky, or create powerful storms to show his power.

Greek culture is also about passion, music, and dance! One of the most emotional Greek dances is **Zeibekiko (Ζεϊμπέκικο)**, a solo dance where the dancer expresses deep feelings through slow, deliberate movements. Unlike other Greek dances, there are no set steps, just pure emotion that comes from feeling the beat of the music and moving accordingly.

And when it comes to embracing life, no one did it better than **Zorba (Ζορμπάς)**, the free-spirited character from **Zorba the Greek**, who taught the world the Greek way of living with joy, resilience, and an incredible love for life.

From Athens to Zorba

From Athens to Zorba, we've explored the rich and exciting world of Greek culture!

Whether it's the ancient myths of the Greek gods, the breathtaking islands like Santorini, the delicious flavors of souvlaki and spanakopita, or the joyful sound of the bouzouki, Greece is a land full of history, tradition, and passion.

But Greek culture is about more than just stories and food, it's about family, hospitality, and a love for life.

Whether you have Greek roots or just a love for this amazing country and culture, we hope this book has helped you discover what it truly means to be Greek.

Greek Alphabet

The Greek alphabet has been used for thousands of years and even helped inspire the English alphabet. From Alpha to Omega, these are the letters Greeks use to read, write, and pass down their history.

		English sound equivalent			English sound equivalent
Αα	alpha	a	Νν	nu	n
Ββ	beta	b	Ξξ	xi	x
Γγ	gamma	g	Οο	omicron	o
Δδ	delta	d	Ππ	pi	p
Εε	epsilon	e	Ρρ	rho	rh r
Ζζ	zeta	z	Σσς	sigma	s
Ηη	eta	ē	Ττ	tau	t
Θθ	theta	th	Υυ	upsilon	y u
Ιι	iota	i	Φφ	phi	ph
Κκ	kappa	k	Χχ	chi	kh
Λλ	lambda	l	Ψψ	psi	ps
Μμ	mu	m	Ωω	omega	ō

– Ευχαριστώ!

(That means "Thank You" in Greek!)

This book was made with lots of love for Greece and for all the families who want to celebrate their heritage or discover something new.

Thank you to everyone who helped bring this book to life, especially "The Band" (Emily, Eleni and Kate) who encouraged me, helped with the content, were my second pair of eyes and, through the years, their legendary spirit and love for Greek culture lifted mine alongside it. Thank you to Androulla Xarras, who helped with the some of the illustrations. To my parents, my grandparents, my family and my friends here and in Greece, and to every Greek and Sunday School teacher I've ever had and every Greek Orthodox priest I've ever met, thank you for instilling in me a deep love for Greece, our religion and our beautiful culture. Your stories, traditions, and support inspired every page. This book is a celebration of our shared heritage, and I couldn't have created it without you.

If this book made you smile with a fond memory or taught you or your child something new about Greek culture, I would be so grateful if you share that with a friend and even more grateful, if you left a review on Amazon. Your review can help other families find the book and join the journey through the ABC's of Being Greek!

www.ingramcontent.com/pod-product-compliance
Lightning Source LLC
Chambersburg PA
CBHW061155030426
42337CB00002B/19